WAKING-UP-UNAFRAID

Ayesha Saunders

ISBN 978-1-63885-557-6 (Paperback)
ISBN 978-1-63885-558-3 (Digital)

Covenant Books, Inc.
11661 Hwy 707
Murrells Inlet, SC 29576
www.covenantbooks.com

Contents

Acknowledgments

Writing this book was not only a lifelong dream, but it was an inspiration for me. It allowed me to be able to talk, learn, and be concerned about people's well-being, which strengthened my prayer life. Writing this book allowed me to learn more about friends, strangers, family, and especially my son. My son has inspired me in so many ways, it would be difficult to list them all. He would ask me often, "Did you finish writing your book?" not in an annoying way but in a persuasive way. You can learn so much from the people you think should be learning from you. Step in their shoes, and begin to live not through them but with them. I try to tell him often how important and an inspiration he is in my life. Don't forget to tell those people how important they are to you while you can and while they can digest your true feelings. Even if they are the reason why you are waking up afraid, maybe by telling them this vital information, you may just learn how to wake up unafraid.

Introduction

The smell of spring, the changing of the leaves that brings on the season of fall, the crisp feeling of the beginning days of winter, and the smell of the ocean during summer—there's nothing like experiencing and appreciating the changing of the seasons. Yes, I have to say that I am a fan of the seasons. Taking that breath in, smiling when life does not seem to permit it, but leaning on the notion that life will get better. Trying to choose your battles wisely is the truth to not worrying about things you have no control over but controlling the things that you do. So, I don't have to worry about worrying about it. The meaning of this phrase can be both complex and simple, in controlling what you are worrying about. The explanation may come during the reading of this book, after the book is done, or during a time in life where you experience an unawakening experience and realize that you can gain control over it or need to just want to gain control over it. Everyone has their journey and their own story. Thank God we were made uniquely different. I have been blessed to have met so many different people; mothers, fathers, friends, coworkers, sons, or daughters, they all had their own stories to tell—stories that would make you laugh or cry; make you want to go to the next level or fall back a little. One thing in common that they all had was a story or time that they woke up afraid. The key is to learn how to wake up unafraid.

Chapter 1

In the Beginning

I started this chapter with a phrase that so many of us are used to hearing. You may hear this phrase and think of many things. I am not about to get that deep, maybe because I don't want to, maybe I can't, or maybe because I don't want people to associate this book with a "religious" situation that can only be understood by someone who attends church frequently, or who knows certain phrases from the Bible, like "I am God, the God of your father; do not be afraid" (Genesis 46:3). This book is not meant to give you an answer but to help you come up with a game plan, or better yet, it should help you learn. Isn't that what life teaches us? Once you learn more about yourself, you learn what not to do. At least that is what we hope; if not, we hope to recognize the aspects of ourselves. So with that, I am going to let you decide what that phrase means to you. After all, you are working on you. You need to learn how to wake up unafraid.

Several television shows pull me in, especially the shows that have a story behind them to teach you something or to make you think—shows that you can relate to or make you want to relate to them. Maybe it is a show that brings up some experience or someone else's experience that you went through with them—television shows that are based on past experiences that seem to show up at the worst moment (kind of like a dream or a nightmare). Usually, we decipher if it's a dream or a nightmare depending on the anxiety or euphoria, you may have experienced. Some experiences can have happened within your lifetime or before you were born. Have you ever had someone tell you about a time that you put yourself in the event? It seems so real, maybe like you were there or you had a window and could put yourself into insight. You may categorize this as having a nightmare or vision or a dream.

There are several definitions of a nightmare that could be researched through multiple streams. In one instance, I found that it states a nightmare could be a frightening or unpleasant dream, or a nightmare can be defined as a terrifying or very unpleasant experience, or another definition defines it as a prospect, a person, thing, or situation that is very difficult to deal with. That can be easily relatable for me.

In the Bible, it states "that in the beginning God created heaven and earth and the earth was without form and void, and darkness was at the face of the deep. And the spirit of God moved upon the face of the waters. And God said. Let there be light: and there was light. And God saw the light, that it was good." Wow, I believe the Bible is there not only to guide us but also to lead us. If God analyzes what he saw, by taking a look at what he created and saw that it was without form, why shouldn't we? I believe there is a message that needs to guide us and prompt us to reanalyze our situations to wake up unafraid. Read deeper into the lesson at hand. Look at your life, and create something that will bring some form to it, happiness, and pleasantries.

Chapter 2

Thoughts

What good is a good life if I am worried about things I can't control? The goal is learning how to deal with what is causing you not to move mentally, spiritually, emotionally, or sometimes physically from that circumstance. That circumstance has a grasp on you, and you do not even realize it, or maybe we just don't want to deal with it. News flash: if you don't deal with certain things, most likely, it will get worse before it gets better. That is why when dealing with certain situations, there are stages. Moving from one stage to the next could either be a goal or be detrimental. Most of the time, it depends on how you are dealing with the circumstance.

My backyard is one of my serene places. It used to be my balcony. I believe we all should have several places where we can learn how to stop, think, and say, "How can we fix this?" Funny, it could even be a phone call or a meetup with someone whom you trust to either listen or give you their opinion that is going to help you to destress the current situation. As I went to my backyard in the dead of night, when silence was more than just hearing the nighttime creatures, *Do the Lord knows what?*

It seemed that the thoughts in my head were moving louder than the sounds of the night. But then I began to ask myself, *Which one am I more afraid of?* So, I stood up, did an about-face, and walked inside, locked the door, and stared out the glass door for another five minutes like something was going to finally appear. Pay attention to what is controlling your fear. It might be the milestone you need to overcome—for me, to be in control of that situation. I believe I chose my battle that night wisely. Bye, nightly critters and animals of the night.

When you don't deal with certain situations, they seem to pile higher and higher or get worse and worse. It may be the assignment that I have to get out, the teacher whom I have to talk to, or what I am going to cook. Some of these things seem so trivial, but what if that is not what is racking your mind? What if it is the thought of, *If he is going to come home drunk, will I be able to spend another day with him before he or she dies, or would I have a job tomorrow?*

I have heard so many stories, throughout the years, from people who were not that much different than you and I. Their occupation may be different, the worrying may be different, and the way they wake up unafraid may be even different, but the key is for us all to get to that point of waking up unafraid.

I have a friend who once screamed the phrase, "You don't understand. You have not been there or witnessed it!"

People most often walk on pins and needles, not knowing what to say when someone is going through a difficulty. If they are looking for comfort, just know that it may seem hard right now, but in time, things will get better. I also let them know that in the same way I am talking to them, maybe they will be on the reverse side. Remember that even though you have not experienced the same path, it does not mean that the person never woke up unafraid. I believe that the fears that life throws at you make you stronger. Now it is up to you to look at it that way. Yes, that is how I look at it. What doesn't kill you will make you stronger. Control your thoughts; don't let your thoughts control you. How do you do that, you ask? Find your happy spot, someone, something, or some place that made you laugh uncontrollably—something I can't do for you. That is why I said, you are working on you.

Chapter 3

Connections

There are so many triumphs (the joy or exultation of victory or success), obstacles (something that *impedes* progress or achievement), stories (an account of incidents or events), and victories (achievement of mastery or success in a struggle or endeavor against odds or difficulties) that we all face in our very unique ways. Those are what make us so different. These words do not define us, but they should empower us. I was told that twins can often feel when the other one is in pain, scared, or hurt, among other relatable tasks, but one thing I was told that is different: the feeling that the other one has. A twin once told me that they had gotten bitten by a stingray. He told me that he felt something, but it was not the pain that the other twin felt. It was a sense—a feeling. It makes you wonder. In Genesis 2:21 (KJV), it reads, "And the Lord God caused a deep sleep to fall upon Adam, and he slept and he took one of his ribs and closed up the flesh instead thereof." It makes you think, *Are we all connected even though we are truly not the same?* Connections through our life experiences.

If you think about it, how are millions of people able to read or hear God's written Word, and once it is preached to us, thousands of people could say, "That was for me"?

Understanding that through this connection, we may be able to use some of the same techniques to get out of various situations. My journey begins with the key question: what do you need to do to wake up unafraid? I want to begin by beginning with several short stories. You may have fallen into this situation at one time or another, or you may know someone who has. While you are reading this, I ask for you to think about some key questions.

1. Could this relate to you in one way or the other?
2. Did you ever try to help a person with a similar situation?
3. What caused my or this person's anxiety or uneasiness?
4. What should I or the person have done differently?
5. What would I do in a similar situation?

My prayer is whoever reads this book not just puts it down and realizes that it was a good book but picks it up with the plan to conquer whatever is keeping them from realizing their potential happiness.

Chapter 4

Focus

In 2018, I could remember, driving to church, and I had so much on my mind. I prayed hard and long and fasted every week. Right in front of me, traffic just stopped, and I came to a halt. When I looked in front of me, there was a car, and it was a Ford Focus. At prayer, on that Thursday, I prayed that God would help me to focus on him and leave trivial things alone. I call things trivial when I feel that I am going about it in the wrong way to handle a situation (of little value or importance). Not that the situation could be so small, but I am handling it like it is. No, I don't believe in the case of losing your job and looking for another as trivial. I call doubting yourself that you will never find a good job as trivial; you are praying but continuing to worry. I am not talking about worrying about your child's well-being but losing sleep and rest because the thoughts overtake your rest. Pray about the situation, and do something about it. Maybe find a group that the child could get into. Start taking them to church, allowing them to hear positive feedback instead of negative. Speak blessings into their life, not curses over their life. If you look into a mirror and do nothing about the reflection in it, then what is the point of looking in the mirror?

I have a friend whom I have known for many years. His story sums up where the near ending is more like the beginning. Sometimes, you may feel that you have been on a roller-coaster ride for so long, you are looking for your breakthrough. There was a time where your life was going so well; you had a lovely family, beautiful children, and great friends. You still didn't feel at ease because you are constantly pulled in so many different directions. You want to be known as part of the fellas, but you want to be a good father and man. You make the choice to feed your flesh. You decide to spend time with your friends who are not living the life you are trying to accomplish, but you're young, and you think time is on your side. You like who you are while you are with your friends. It is temporary but enough to get you through the days ahead. It has come to the point where you are not spending time growing yourself or your ideas. Things start to spiral out of control, but it didn't just start that way. You just began to start noticing. A leak sometimes starts small, then it begins to get bigger and bigger. Now your job is in jeopardy; you are contemplating quitting. You don't sit down and come up with a plan, or so you think. You decide to go back to school or look for a better job. The only thing is, it is a little harder now—not impossible—but when a wooden board sits in the elements for a long time and it is not treated, it can get weak. That is when the structure needs support. At this time, he is spending less time sleeping because his life seems unbearable. He is constantly waking up at three or four in the morning. He still does not know how to get a hold of it. He starts to blame other people for his problems: coworkers, friends, children, and even parents (sounds familiar). Stories change, but they stay the same. Temporary happiness is not going to solve the problem of waking up un-afraid. Learning how to get to the level of knowing that your plan has to be bigger than temporary satisfaction is the key to seeing it through it.

I heard this story about this lady who decided to quit church, and she told her pastor that she is quitting church because of all of the heathens, back biters, and mean people (I am so paraphrasing this, LOL). Her pastor told her, next week, to carry a glass of water around the church without letting it spill and report back to him. When asked, she said that she was so focused on not letting the water spill that she didn't notice the people. The moral of the story is what you are focused on will not allow you to have time for the other distractions. So, focus on the positives in your life, and you will learn to let go of the things you thought were important. Nightmares need to be fed. Are you feeding the things that are taking your energy, time, and sleep away?

Chapter 5

Growth

Sitting in my backyard, I started to laugh because it was so funny how we do things and don't even realize that key things of our life are made up of our actions. I had six trees that I brought for my backyard. I planted them and waited a whole year. No progress. I asked my son, "Does it look like the trees are growing?"

He responded, "I haven't paid attention to them."

I waited a couple of more weeks, pulled them up, brought some new ones, and replanted them. I waited a year, and the same thing. But this time, my patience had grown in so many different ways. I had been through some things and got that *ahaa* moment. I saw the possibility that if I change the way of my thinking and do things a little different, I will begin to see the growth in...(replace the dots, where you need to see growth). I wanted a full tree, within a little time, but not allowing time to see the tree grow. I know from starting a garden, there are stages that a tree would need to go through for me to reap its full productivity. Trees, as well as plants, need space to grow, water, sun, and nutrients. Funny when we go to the doctor, how many times do they say that we are lacking in one thing or the next?

When I planted my tree, it was a baby plant or a sapling, a small tree that can be between one and four inches in diameters. Now I thought that because I purchased the small tree, I was out of the woods, but as I learned, it required just as much time and energy as planting a seed, if not more. As I learned, it encountered similar threats as if it was a seed. The soil had to be right. You had to give it water but not too much. The temperature and the amount of sun it received among other things had to be right. As I began to look over my life and think about how things could be better, I tend to ask myself, *What do I need to do in order to grow?* I realize it could be a couple of factors, good food, spiritual growth, or maybe a good relationship. I was told time and time again that having a plan is good, but what if the plan failed? Where do you go? What do you turn to, or whom do you turn to? Sometimes, those plans have your mind wondering, and especially when it fails, your worrying may turn into regret. I have found that not many people can pick up the pieces. In fact, sometimes, they can make the pieces impossible to locate to put them back together again. That is when you need to have a strategy. I don't look at a strategy as walking away and forgetting it, but I look at a strategy as trying to get some results. One of the definitions of a strategy is a plan of action or policy designed to achieve a major or overall aim. I like to aim for the prize, especially if the prize is allowing me to sleep better at night or waking up unafraid.

Chapter 6

Sleeping With Your Eyes Open

As I walked to the restaurant that was located in my hotel, I contemplated if I should go back to my hotel room to eat my breakfast. The restaurant was set up like a typical hotel restaurant, and I realized that my schedule was off already. So, I decided to order my breakfast to go, in order to multitask. Since I was already behind my propelled allotted time for the day, I decided I could kill two birds with one stone: I will eat, get dressed, and watch a little television. I looked around the dining room and noticed that a gentleman was sitting at one of the tables. His breakfast was almost finished, and there was another table that was occupied by a man and a lady. The lady spoke by saying hi. I realized that was enough to make up my mind—politeness—something I was not expecting since I am always the one to speak first to strangers (I find that it lightens the atmosphere, like the atmosphere is heavy). When the waiter approached me and asked me if I would be taking my breakfast to my room, I told him, "I will have it to stay."

I found a table that was in view of the television. As my food came out, I noticed a couple of things not to my liking. Isn't that how it happens a lot? One bad thought or attitude brings on one and then two, and before you know it, it seems like a funk you can't seem to shake off. My food was cold. The wheat bread didn't taste like wheat. So now my thoughts are that he thinks that I didn't notice that the bread was not wheat. So, I called him over and let him know that my food was cold, and I slipped in, "By the way, this bread tastes more like rye than wheat."

He apologized, took away my plate, and asked me if I want coffee.

I thought, *Of course I do. Why didn't you ask me when I first came in.*

I still didn't realize that my emotions were making me feel more of a sense of unpleasantness. How to control this anger? What I was feeling was making me seem afraid not of the situation but of my impending thoughts to make me think the worst. He brought my plate back warm and a slice of rye bread to show me the difference.

I thought, *I just made things worse. Now he thinks I do not know what rye bread looks like.*

I told him that I am used to wheat bread not having big pieces of wheat, and it was hard, knowing that it was the maker of the bread, not the waiter. Understand that life is not about you knowing everything, but you allow yourself to grow out of every situation. I apologized and began to have small talk with him. As I started drinking my coffee, I decided to ask the gentleman who was sitting across from me rather if he was here for business or vacation.

He told me, "Both."

He began to explain his line of work. He worked as a match agent for boxers. He told me that he used to be a boxer himself, but he started working within the banking industry. I told him that changing to that line of work was interesting. For someone to change career decisions from being a banker to becoming a boxer was unique. He told me that he does it, and it gets guys off of the street, so he felt good about what he does. He also told me that a couple of months ago, one of his guys died from fighting on the way to the hospital. He recalled that it was hard for him. That was one of the times where he slept with his eyes open. I asked him did he over come it and if so, what did he do to overcome it. He explained that if he did not do it, more would be lost than just that one. He explained that knowing what he was doing was more than helping himself but helping to get young kids off of the street, which makes him sleep at night, he eventually, came to that realization. I realized that his answer to his waking up unafraid is more controlled by letting go of the things that you have no control over. Life is inevitable that way. If you can make an imprint, would you? Doing good does not guarantee that you will not experience waking up unafraid, but it can be a shot to knowing that you can go back to sleep, knowing that you tried to counteract the negative aspects with more positive aspects.

Chapter 7

Waking Up

Waking up feels good when you get a good sleep. But what if your sleep was broken? What if you woke up sweating or breathing for air? What are you supposed to do? I could tell you what I do, but that will not necessarily help you. You often hear people say that "when you get ready for bed, have a good ritual." I have this friend whose ritual consists of food and sleeping medicine. That is not something that I would recommend since I do believe that food needs time to digest properly, and I do not agree with sleeping medicine since it may be a temporary solution or have different side effects that can impact your body. I was told by some people this is the only way they are able to stay asleep the whole night through. If you have younger kids or a very event-filled schedule, that does not let up or get easier, your sleep is often interrupted. I believe your body, mind, and spirit should be in tune together. If your body is not in tune with your spirit, I believe that is a key decision for you to readjust that schedule or plan. You know as they say, if one way doesn't work, try another way. You should also find what works best for you. If you are generally a person that is always cold, make your sleep area comfortable for you. If you always find that it is hot, then vice versa. Find a comfortable bedtime ritual that would ensure peace during your sleep time. Also, I find that a ritual can be praying/meditating before you go to sleep—learning how to bring calmness to the ending or beginning of your day. Not all lives are orchestrated the same way. Some people need to sleep during the day, and some need to sleep during the night, but neither one of us want to wake up afraid. So, we all have to learn how to combat it.

I have found that one way to combat stress is to think of things that keep you calm.

Chapter 8

Channeling Your Thoughts

Another story that might relate to you is being in love. Sometimes, it feels like the greatest experience on earth, especially when it is during the good times. You finish each other's sentences and smile at each other when the other person notices it. Your family gets along (well, at least some of them). You spend time just thinking about the other person during the day and cannot wait to speak to them again. Time passes, and the love that you once felt is not felt anymore. People have told you that marriage is work, but you were never told this is the type of work that is required. Your partner starts to come home late. The family looks at you in a strange, unusual type of way when you come around. Things have defiantly changed. But you were told it is a work in progress. But you don't want to work at this. The screaming matches become physical; you want to leave, but where would you go? You have children whom you are responsible for. Hope is gone. It seems like you have given up, but something has got to change. You find hope in family and friends. They tell you to leave but do not give you any way out. The nightmares are beginning; you find yourself waking up afraid. You desperately want this pain to stop. You want to learn how to end this living nightmare and how to wake up unafraid.

As a teenager, I suffered from headaches. The headaches became so deliberating that I was told to think of things that relaxed me. Ironically, some advice can come from people who learn how to deal with obstacles that they once overcame or is trying to overcome. I would take deep breaths and think of a place I wanted to go or have been. I would think of details about that place. By visualizing down to the tiniest detail, I was able to forget about my headache. I still needed medical attention. It allowed me to not focus on my headaches during some moments and distract my mind from focusing on the pain. That could also be a key to waking up unafraid. Visualize beautiful scenery that relaxes you—something that gives you the peace that could surpass all under-standing. I'm not a doctor; therefore, I am not telling you to self-diagnose yourself. Make sure you seek a medical professional when it comes to your health—understanding that there are certain situations that you can control and certain situations that are out of your control. Please know the difference.

Chapter 9

Positioned

When you go through a situation where it seems impossible to overcome, realize that no matter how hard, scary, or impossible the battle we have to face, we know we have someone in our corner. In Mathew 26-27 (AMPC) it reads, Look at the birds of the air; they neither sow nor reap nor gather into barns, and yet your heavenly Father keeps feeding them. Are you not worth much more than they?

> [27]And who of you by worrying *and* being anxious can add one unit of measure (cubit) to his stature *or* to the [b]span of his life?

Position yourself at that moment in time where the outcome is a reward. How do you do that, you ask? Live for now. You have to realize that most of the time, you're in the process of developing your outcome. And remember to change your vision to see things in a positive position. There is so much you can learn through life. It just depends if you see what you have gone through as a lesson or a *lesser*. Live in peace with yourself knowing that what is in front of you is better than what is behind you, having the peace and understanding to conquer life, but having the attitude that you are growing through this, and you will come out a victor. Position yourself so that your next move is going to impact your next move.

Chapter 10

Nightmares

Having a new event in your life is scary. It is a blessing because you never know where it is going to lead you. Possibly it could make you a stronger father, mother, wife, husband, child, teacher, believer, or worker. The list can go on and on; you can fill in the blank. I would wake up in the middle of the night, searching for my child. I could laugh now because it began when he was just a newborn. But it never stopped, and I was told that it will never stop. I wonder if it was because I was a single parent, being fearful I felt, I was not equipped to care for another human besides myself. Or it is because I was not able to maintain a marriage with a husband who left me and my baby to fend for ourselves. Understand that I have heard so many stories of women and men residing in different types of households and they had a different type of fear, but they still experienced fear. One of the deepest fears is when a mother's child would be taken from her from an unfortunate event, no matter what that event may be. Now my son is a young adult, and when he is out late I often stay up wondering if he is okay. I, sometimes fall asleep by a mistake, and I blame myself because I wake up afraid. Fearing that the unthinkable will happen, I ask myself, *Would it ever stop?*

I have friends who have lost their children, in many different circumstances. You ask yourself, *Do they ever get over it? Or learn to wake up unafraid.*

I believe no, it's not something that you can get over. Even though life goes on, the thought of that person will always be there. Grief sometimes never goes away, it becomes bearable. "For when I am weak then I am strong" (2 Corinthians 12:10). This is my way of waking up unafraid. I realize that this burden is too hard to bear by myself, and I lean on God for understanding. Understanding for what I don't understand, he understands so much more. It has been over twenty years later, and I am still feeling the death of my mother. Sometimes, it comes with tears, sometimes just a memory of things we did together. Sometimes, I think if I would have done certain things differently. God lets me know, in so many different situations, that he got this.

There are so many passages in the Bible about not becoming afraid while sleeping. These are a few of my favorites:

A stone was brought and placed over the mouth of the

den, and the king sealed it with his own signet ring and with the rings of his nobles, so that Daniel's situation might not be changed. Then the king returned to his palace and spent the night without eating and without any entertainment being brought to him. And he could not sleep. (Daniel 6: 17–18)

But you, LORD, are a shield around me, my glory, the One who lifts my head high. I call out to the LORD, and he answers me from his holy mountain. I lie down and sleep; I wake again, because the LORD sustains me. I will not fear though tens of thousands assail me on every side. (Psalm 33: 3–6)

Imagine worrying about the inevitable and not being able to change your thoughts. Or imagine worrying about something but deciding because you have no control over it, you are going to trust that God will work it out for you. I love this passage of the Bible, where David is talking to God, convincing himself that God is a shield around him. I realize that life is not just about accepting God but knowing that he has the best for you—knowing that you are protected, no matter what situation you are facing.

Chapter 11

Don't Give Up

Waking up not scared, angry, or confused, but waking up knowing how you are going to handle the day that's in front of you. For as long as I could remember, I felt I had to prove something to myself. I can do it. With God's grace, I can do it. You have to get to the point where your bite is bigger than your bark. I always felt that I would do something, read something, or say something to get what I needed. In the end, I always had to let it go. Don't give up. Your fight is never over, until you say it is over. And I have decided that my bite is a continuation of me. Don't let your bark be louder than your fight. There will be times when you think it's your time to sit back, that maybe the time to fight, and when you think you have to fight, you may have to sit back. Consult with God to order to order your steps. Being confident that when prayers are going up, it's time to pray for yourself and for someone else. Ephesians 6:18

(AMP) With all prayer and petition pray [with specific requests] at all times [on every occasion and in every season] in the Spirit, and with this in view, stay alert with all perseverance and petition [interceding in prayer] for all [a]God's people.

Fasting

My fasting comes at a time when it just seems right to do it. When I need to sit back and let God do the fighting, that's my fast. Some people meditate, fast, concentrate, or be still. I say wrap it all in one. We are facing times in our lives when we have to decipher God for ourselves and as David said in the Bible (we have to make it personal like it was written specifically for us). I realized God will talk to us on an individual basis. Sometimes, I do a group fast with people, and I get so excited, even when I realize God just spoke to me. Sometimes, it has nothing to do with what I was fasting for or praying about, but God has a message for me or someone else, and I am thankful for the messages. We live in a world where acronyms are used often. My acronym for fighting at still times is FAST, which means "fighting at still times."

> And when they had ordained them elders in every church, and had prayed with fasting, they commended them to the Lord, on whom they believed. (Acts 14:23 KJV)

Gifts

We have to give/take our gifts and don't look back. That is what faith is—letting God explain your gifts through his means, trusting and believing that "the race is not to the swift or the battle to the strong, nor does food come to the wise or wealth to the brilliant or favor to the learned; but time and chance happen to them all." This is written from *Ecclesiastes 9:11*. I have read many books, and I try to find the message in all of them. I make sure it's a message that I could use; rather, it's for myself or someone else.

A spiritual gift is given to each of us so we can help each other. To one person the Spirit gives the ability to give wise advice; to another the same Spirit gives a message of special knowledge. The same Spirit gives great faith to another, and to someone else the one Spirit gives the gift of healing. He gives one person the power to perform miracles, and another the ability to prophesy. He gives someone else the ability to discern whether a message is from the Spirit of God or from another spirit. Still another person is given the ability to speak in unknown languages, while another is given the ability to interpret what is being said.

It is the one and only spirit who distributes all these gifts. He alone decides which gift each person should have. (1 Corinthians 12:8–11 NLT)

Mind over Matter

You have to change the way you think to change the way you feel. We all have a story, and that story can either defeat you or make you stronger.

Is any among you afflicted? Let him pray. Is any merry? Let him sing psalms. (James 5:13 KJV)

Everyone Is Different

Everyone is different and has their own story to narrate. Don't think that because it worked for you, a friend, or a loved one, then the color will never change. Have you ever washed clothes that were supposed to be all washed in the same wash as you were instructed, but something with a different color came out of the washing machine? There are forty-eight crayons in a large box of crayons. Take two or three or more of those crayons and begin to overlap the colors. Now, you have more colors than you started out knowing about. Understand that your story is unique, but your story is not so unique that other colors won't experience a similar situation. Accept the other colors and the stories that they may share.

Guilty Expression

We have all come to a point where our loved ones are embarrassed about what we say or do. It can become so easy for us to lash out and become defensive. We may think that we are doing a disservice to the other person by not lashing out. But are we doing a disservice to God? We have to be careful that what we are guarding is not of our heart or our self-esteem. We may be destroying a blessing.

> The tongue has the power
> of life and death, and those who
> love it will eat its fruit. (Proverbs
> 18:21 NKJV)

Chapter 12

The Start of Happiness

My morning prayer starts with a "Good morning, God. Thank you for waking me up and starting me on my day. Thank you for all of the blessings that are going to come my way today. Thank you for the peaceful sleep. Thank you for teaching me that you are the beginning and the ending, Alpha and Omega. Nothing is in hiding from you. Thank you for keeping me in your resting place and me not having any doubt about the care that you have for me. I love you more today and forevermore, in Jesus's name, amen."

Understand that life may throw a lot at you, but when you start with a positive attitude, how can the darts of life pierce you? Starting each day with peace in your life is so important. Don't give up the thought that you can be happy. You have to take a step through every obstacle, every day, every hour, and every minute.

Here is a quick story of me controlling me: One day, I decided to write things down that I repeated every day. Every day, more items got added to the list. Some things were not done every day, but they were repetitive. I would skip one or two days. I began to add columns. Some columns listed why I did it and how I felt after doing it. I began to learn what gives me peace and what makes me anxious. Guess what are some of the things that impact us to wake up afraid? We don't even realize that it may be something that we are doing every day or every other day. It could be as simple as eating after a certain time or watching TV or scrolling through your phone. Learn to control yourself, and place obstacles in the right receptacle of life, and just maybe you will, too, wake up unafraid. One of my favorite verses in the Bible has helped me in so many ways. Try to repeat it before you go to bed and when you wake up.

> The LORD bless you and keep you; the LORD make his face shine on you and be gracious to you; the LORD turn his face toward you and give you peace.
> (Numbers 6:24–26 NIV)

About the Author

Ayesha Saunders grew up in a Pentecostal church in Brooklyn, New York. She was always inquisitive to learn more about why humans think the way they do. She first attended college as a psychology student in Upstate New York and then later switched her bachelor's degree to political science with a concentration in public policy. She is currently earning her Master of Science degree in Charlotte, North Carolina. She understood the importance of surrounding yourself with people whom you can grow with and learn from. She lives by the motto that if she wants to be first, she has to be willing to be the very last. Volunteering her time and doing mission trips are a passion of hers. That began her love for people and writing. This is her first published book.